Anxiety Soothers©

Visualizations,
Activities
&
Body Cues

for a
Peaceful Day
and a
Good Night's Sleep

by Jeremy Cole, MSW, LCSW

www.anxietysoothers.com

INFORMAT

To
Gabriel, Laurie and Isla (I-la)
who make me smile-ah,
and to Eric.

My Dear Friend, Welcome to Anxiety Soothers!

I call you 'friend', even though we have never met, because I imagine my arm around your shoulder and yours around mine as we face together this hard topic. Herein are gathered my favorite *Visualizations*, *Activities* and *Body Cues* for a peaceful day and a good night's sleep.

Anxiety Soothers contains twenty *Visualizations*, *Activities* and *Body Cues* for a total of 60 healthy resources that you can call upon, right now, to counter the negative effects of anxiety. *Visualizations* engage your imagination, *Activities* draw upon your problem-solving skills and *Body Cues* ground you in physical awareness. To further assist the anxiety easing process, **Anxiety Soothers** is color-coded. The *Information* pages that start and finish the book are framed in blue, *Visualizations* in **purple**, *Activities* in orange and *Body Cues* in green. **Anxiety Soothers** combines text (left hemisphere) with graphics (right hemisphere) so that your beautiful brain is fully engaged. The one-resource-per-page format enables you to focus on one resource at a time, which s-l-o-w-s down the feverish pace of anxiety and allows easy entry of fresh information.

Set aside ten minutes to help yourself. Prop open the book and read a page. Let the words and visuals sink in as you take a deep breath. Involve your senses by letting yourself see, taste, smell, hear and feel a *Visualization*. Use a pen and paper, or computer keyboard, to **do** an *Activity*. Focus on appreciation for your physical body as you absorb a *Body Cue*. If a particular *Visualization*, *Activity* or *Body Cue* works even a little, **take note**. When you are dealing with an emotion as formidable as anxiety, even the tiniest bit of relief is an indication of positive potential. Your goal is to develop that potential. To that end…

Consider your mind as an invisible set of muscles. The *worry* (and maybe the *self-critical*) muscle is well developed: Rambo-esque. The *centering* or *calming* muscle is puny with disuse. With practice, you will build up the centering and calming muscle and thus gain skill at redirecting your mind away from frightening and worrying thoughts. The Rambo muscle will dwindle as you put your energy elsewhere.

This practice is key to reducing anxiety. Anxiety derives its strength from fear, and fear is an emotion that feeds upon itself. It spreads through your system like water spilled on a flat surface. The three different approaches in **Anxiety Soothers**: *Visualizations*, *Activities* and *Body Cues*, invite your entire being to get involved in the anxiety-relieving process. What's more, they are **fast**, virtually **free** and **without side-effects**.

Set gentle goals for yourself (one page per day? per week?) as you use **Anxiety Soothers** so that 'performance pressure' does not become part of your stress. Consider practicing soothing exercises for five minutes when you are fairly calm so that they seem familiar when you really need them. Remember that gaining strength in the invisible realm of *emotion* is similar to shaping up at a gym: you will notice progress with practice and over time. Soon your anxiety will be reduced and contained—like water in a big bowl by the kitchen sink. Imagine emptying that bowl down the drain…

Wishing you the blessings of peace of mind.

INFORMATION

Anxiety: Definition and Symptoms

Anxiety is defined in Random House Webster's Unabridged Dictionary (2001) as "1. distress or uneasiness of mind caused by fear of danger or misfortune"… Anxiety symptoms fall along the spectrum of the "fear" responses: fight, flight or freeze. Any experiences from the following list are common—although, thank goodness, they rarely occur all at once.

- **Breathing**: rapid, shallow, gasping, holding breath, fear of choking.
- **Heart**: racing, pounding, palpitations, chest pain, fear of a heart attack.
- **Digestion**: fluttering or sinking feeling in stomach, nausea, vomiting, intestinal cramps, diarrhea.
- **Sensation**: tingling in extremities; dry mouth, difficulty swallowing, feeling chilled, sweaty or overheated and/or dizzy, lightheaded or faint; feeling 'unreal' or as if you've left your body.
- **Mentally**: thoughts racing, unable to think clearly or mind "blank", irritable, escalation of phobias (snakes, spiders, heights, etc); catastrophic, repetitive thoughts (it's hopeless!), fear of going crazy, fear of dying.
- **Behavior**: stammering, shaking, trembling, twitching, tics, jumpy, flushing red, turning pale, easily tearful, overeating or unable to eat, frequent urination, disturbed sleep.
- **Musculature**: neck tension, back pain, overall tightness in muscles.

Sprinkled throughout life in brief doses, anxiety supplies bursts of energy to get through challenging events and calls attention to iffy situations we might otherwise ignore. Anxiety may be laced with excitement, as before an important date or a performance. It is, of itself, positive in its contribution *unless its severity or chronicity interferes with life.*

TABLE OF CONTENTS

Visualizations: Description

V-1 Rubbish
V-2 Safe
V-3 The Worrier
V-4 The Judge
V-5 Napoleon's Bureau
V-6 Restful Scene
V-7 Cool the Brain
V-8 Just Passing Through
V-9 Step Away
V-10 Internal Smile
V-11 Pleasant Lists
V-12 Engine Adjustment
V-13 I.T., Sleep!
V-14 Turn It Over
V-15 Under the Radar
V-16 Taming the Task
V-17 Dust Bunnies
V-18 Warm and Relaxed
V-19 Coast
V-20 To the Moon!

Activities: Description

A-1 Anxiety Journaling
A-2 Rational/ Irrational
A-3 Contain It
A-4 A Date to Worry
A-5 Relax Muscles
A-6 Listen
A-7 Pizza, Anyone?
A-8 Three Good Things
A-9 Laugh It Off
A-10 Forgive
A-11 Aargh!
A-12 Walk and Talk
A-13 Anyone There?
A-14 Once Upon a Time
A-15 Good Things Journal
A-16 Preparation Activities
A-17 Observe and Accept
A-18 The "Not" List
A-19 Keeping it Real
A-20 Active Meditation

INFORMATION

Body Cues: Description

B-1   Limit Stimulants
B-2   Be Gentle
B-3   Edit Exposure
B-4   Tension Release
B-5   Massage
B-6   Stretch
B-7   Nutrition
B-8   Exercise
B-9   Before Midnight
B-10 Three-hour Rule
B-11 Sleep Routine
B-12 Natural Sleep Aids
B-13 Soak Your Feet
B-14 Healing Hands
B-15 Slow Down
B-16 Great Grounding
B-17 90 Seconds
B-18 The Nose Knows
B-19 Breathe
B-20 This. Here. Now.

Information

I-1   "Some days, the Dragon wins."
I-2   "Some days, the Dragon wins." Cont.
I-3   Addendum
I-4   Hello, Cynic!
I-5   Psychotherapy and Meditation
I-6   Sympathetic /Parasympathetic
I-7   About the Author and Illustrator
I-8   Anxiety Soothers Website
I-9   Thanks
I-10 Purchasing Information

Visualizations: Description

Visualizations are readily available for use anytime, anywhere, without anyone knowing and at no expense: all you need is your mind! That's right: fast, free, no side-effects and always available. You may be surprised to discover that you are naturally visualizing all the time. Consider these every-day examples:

1. You have a crush on someone at work or in school (usually unattainable) and vividly imagine romance with this person. (Whew!) Your body responds…
2. You watch a scary movie and now you can't get to sleep. You lie there, imagining someone breaking into your home. Your body goes on high alert…
3. Your beloved chum has been away for three lonely months, and you are about to see her. You picture her face and suddenly you are smiling…

Just three to five minutes of *visualizing* creates natural physiological changes in our bodies, which may be **consciously directed** to improve health. ♥ The secret is to engage as many of your five senses as you can (touch, smell, sight, sound, taste) to evoke a full-body experience—the more sensory, the better! As you *live into* the positive images that you are visualizing, you engage your naturally *soothing* parasympathetic nervous system and transform that wild renegade, your mind, into a powerful, cost-free ally. *Ahhhh!*

Spend five focused minutes practicing a *visualization* when you are not in crisis (build the 'muscle') to strengthen its effectiveness in times of need. Use your senses: imagine it is real and incorporate smells, colors, textures, sensations and sounds. Enjoy playing with and personalizing these *visualizations*, and trust your ability to come up with your own. Congratulate yourself, for this is an *excellent* use of your energy and time.

Rubbish

Visualize (or, in your mind's eye, see...) a garbage can. Throw in it all the cluttery details, rehashed conversations, useless gossip, embarrassing memories, self-blaming phrases and negative images that are filling your mental space. Slam down the lid. If they start running through your head again, immediately throw them back into the garbage can. Visualize a garbage truck arriving (ew, the smell!) and a business-like worker picking up the can and tossing all that rubbish into the truck. Listen to that rumble as it drives away.

VISUALIZATIONS

1

Safe

Evaluate the stuff speeding through or clogging your head. It may not all be rubbish; some of it may be important or even sacred to you (i.e., memories of a deceased loved one). *Visualize* storing important material in a protected place. ♥ For example, imagine a large safe (as ornate as you like, maybe in a castle or a field…) and place within it what is important. Close the door and spin the dial, knowing you can come back to it and it is **Safe**. *Visualize* laying sacred material on a white-clothed altar, or whatever image conveys "sacred" to you, and leave it there to be tended by your ideal caregivers (Angels? Priests? Woodland spirits?).

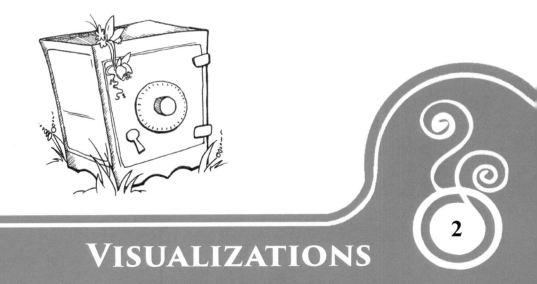

VISUALIZATIONS

The Worrier

Ask yourself, *what does my Worrier self look like?* Try to get some objectivity by (metaphorically speaking) stepping back to look at this aspect of yourself. Is this grown-up me, sitting on a curb with my head dropped onto my folded arms? Am I striding back and forth? Is the *Worry* me a spouting teenager? A needy little kid? *Visualize your worrier self getting what you need:*

💙 Take exhausted *Worrier* to a spa. Imagine safe and loving people (or a person) tucking *Worrier* into a big fluffy bed or, if you prefer, a hammock by the beach. Lay a cool cloth over his or her forehead and feed *Worrier* a light and nourishing soup.
💙 Run agitated *Worrier* back and forth on a beach to get rid of excess energy.
💙 See safe and loving people listening attentively to teenage *Worrier,* and leave them to it.
💙 Rock little child *Worrier* on a safe and comforting lap.

Visualize tending to your Worrier self's needs.

VISUALIZATIONS

The Judge

Is there a *Judge* aspect within you, pointing a finger at you and listing all your faults? If so, tell that part to **Back Off!** Visualize (see yourself) stepping out of the room and closing the door in his or her face. Send him/ her off to lecture to a classroom of interested cows. This *Judge* or *Critic* (some sort of authority figure) might ultimately be well intended (to be further explored...) but it often acts abusively, saying terrible things to your Self. (Ex: "*If you weren't so stupid, you'd....*") When hearing this voice, say firmly:

"Stop! I am not going to abuse my Self."

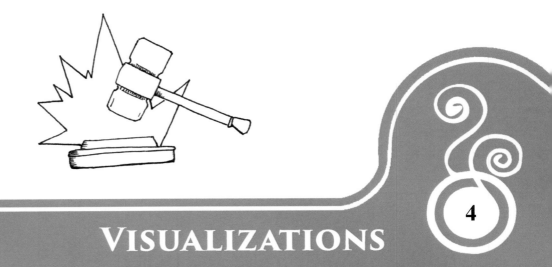

VISUALIZATIONS

Napoleon's Bureau

The story goes that Napoleon used visualization. Every night before he fell asleep, he'd imagine a bureau with many slim drawers, used in his day for storing maps. He would visualize opening the top drawer and putting a concern or issue in it, closing the drawer, and then continuing down to the next one. By the time he'd finished with all the drawers in the bureau, he was ready to sleep. Imagine putting your concerns in the drawers of this bureau, and then shutting them **all** for the night. *Ahh!*

VISUALIZATIONS

Restful Scene

Soothe yourself by imagining a favorite scene, real or unreal. Include cherished sights, sounds, smells, textures and a calming mood. Use your senses to evoke a full body experience.

Example:

      I enter a lovely, quiet, dimly lit room that contains a long pool of clear, revitalizing water. There's a faint hint of my favorite fragrance in the air. I slip out of my clothes and into the water, which is at just the temperature I need. Slowly I swim the length of the pool, feeling my cares wash off of me. I get out and wrap myself in the fluffy soft robe, in my favorite color, which is awaiting me. At this end of the room, there is an ample bed beneath a moonlit window. I climb onto this bed, pull the soft covers up over my shoulders, and rest or sleep in this lovely, safe space, lulled by the gentle sounds of a little waterfall just outside my window.

VISUALIZATIONS

Cool the Brain

If you are having what I call *brain fever*—head hot and clogged with jumbled thoughts—try this humorous image: imagine unscrewing the top of your head, reverently lifting out your brain, going to the sink, and gently running cool water over and through it. Sometimes you might very gently massage it. Then when it is all cooled down, reverently place it back in your skull. You are seeking to interrupt clogged thought patterns and introduce cooling self-care.

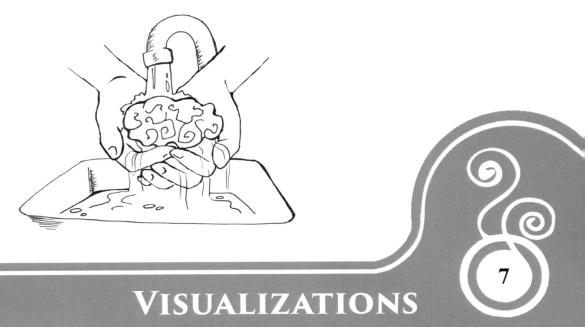

Just Passing Through

Are thoughts racing through your mind? Encourage them to race **through** and not stay. Imagine that you step back, watch the thought race into your head, see it slide across a slippery floor and out the opposite ear. Thoughts are just thoughts—they are not facts. *No matter how much you believe in a thought, it is not real—not unless it is actually happening, right now.* So, no need to get involved in anxious thoughts; they are just passing through. *Bye-bye!*

VISUALIZATIONS

Step Away

A state of mind (worry, anxiety) is simply *a state of mind*—it is not all of who you are, though it can certainly feel like it is. Remind yourself, "*Now I am in my Worry space— but that isn't where I spend my life*." —and then step away from it. Visualize a column of worry within which you are standing, and then step out of it and walk away. Regardless of how you feel while you are in it, there is MORE to you than this *worry* place.

♥ Imagine that you are in a room with your worries, which are little gremlins. You open the door and step out of that room (*ahh!*), closing the door behind you. The little gremlins thump on the door wanting to come with you, but you walk away. Eventually they settle down on the floor, bored, as you get on with your life.

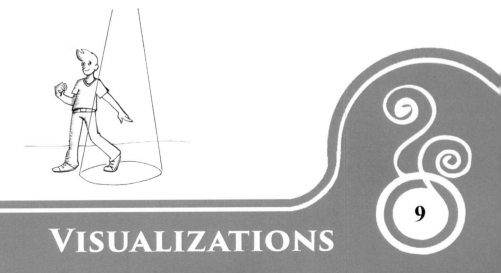

VISUALIZATIONS

Internal Smile

Smile to your different organs. This practice is from Chinese medicine, and is no doubt quite healthy. As you lie in bed with your eyes closed, imagine your heart and smile at it. You may find that your lips actually lift in a little smile. Smile at your brain, your liver, lungs, etc. Do this quietly and slowly, moving through whatever organs come to mind, and appreciating them. After all, they are beavering away all the time, just for you.

"I love you, liver."
"Thank you, lungs!"
"You are so beautiful, heart!"

Pleasant Lists

People find it relaxes them, and takes their mind away from worries, to make simple lists (not related to work) in their head. No doing this 'right' or 'perfect': the goal is to relaxedly please yourself with images you enjoy, using the alphabet to gently keep your mind "on point". For example: all the names for birds that begin with A, then B, then C.... etc. Visualize each bird. All the names of (flowers, tools, vehicles, singers, sport terms) that begin with A, then B, then C.... I do this thinking of positive people I've known in my life whose names begin with A...B...C... haven't met my "X", "Y" or "Z" person yet; could it be you? I visualize each smiling face as I think of the name, and if I don't remember "Bertram" until I'm in the R's—no worries! I'm happy to back-track and add dear Berty to the B's. Keep it loose, keep it simple, keep it relaxed. This is for you.

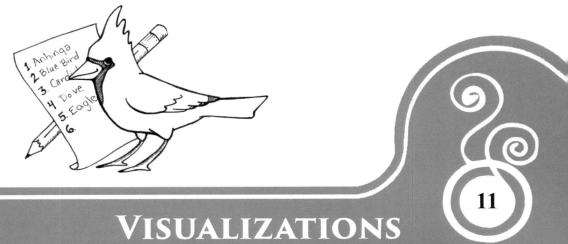

VISUALIZATIONS

Engine Adjustment

Are you racing inside? Do you feel like an engine that is revving too fast? Visualize yourself opening the hood of your car. Turn down the idler, and close the hood. Listen to the quiet, slowed-down sound.

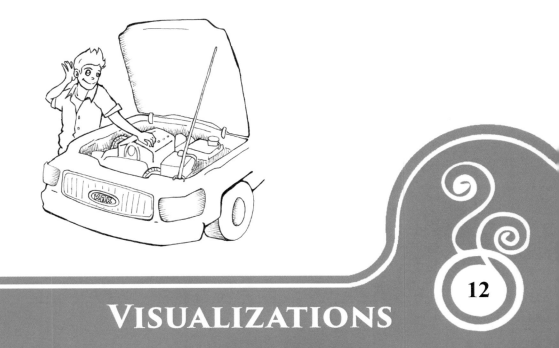

I.T., Sleep!

Who is the "I.T." person in your head, keeping everything so busy up there? (For non-computer people, "I.T." stands for Information Technology.) Initially, mine was an old man on roller skates who dug information out of a vast underground archive of floor-to-ceiling bookshelves. He was good, but slow. Now, in addition, there's a young woman on roller blades who zips among computer terminals in a well-lit room. *Put whoever it is to bed!* Visualize this normally busy part of you (first unlacing and removing your roller skates) pulling back the blankets and gratefully climbing into bed, rolling over, nestling in and sinking into deep sleep. The computers are shut down, the phones are on their chargers, all the lights are out, and it is time to sleep.

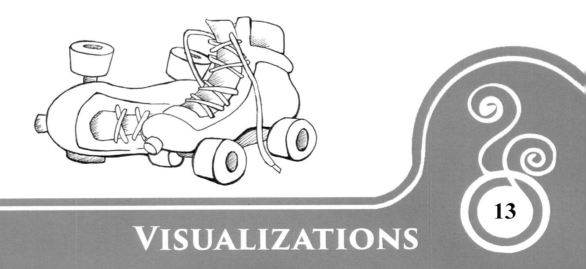

Turn It Over

If you have a spiritual life, actively pray: *"dear God, I am turning it over to you"*. Visualize, or let yourself feel, the load being lifted from you by an all-loving Presence that understands your burdens, and has no need to judge you.

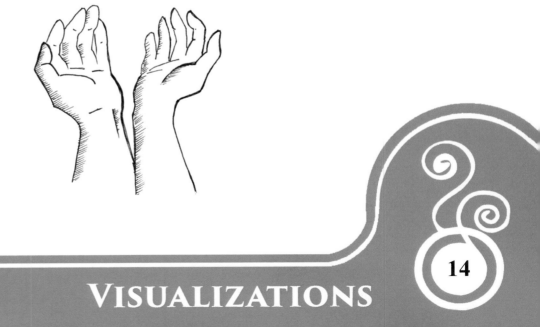

VISUALIZATIONS

Under the Radar

Are thoughts streaming through your head? Is your brain congested with discordant phrases, overwhelming lists and remorseless "shoulds"? Go under the radar. *Visualize* all that brain activity as a stream flowing above your head. You are aware of it, but residing in the rest of you that is under the stream. *(Whew!)*
What if that stream just flowed away, up into the stratosphere? *Ahh!*

Taming the Task

Anxious about a task you must perform? Are you giving a speech, questioning your boss's proposal, standing up for yourself with a dominant relative, speaking your truth to an addicted friend? Use *Visualizations* to prepare yourself in advance:

❤ *Visualize* the panicky part of you, perhaps frazzled and vibrating, bundled off to rest with a nurturing friend/ elder/ healer in a cozy place—i.e., see that part moving aside. *Ahhh!*

❤ Ask yourself, how old do I feel? If you are feeling young and small, your child-self needs protecting. Children get overwhelmed when they try to do grown-up jobs! *Visualize* sending your child self to a delightful playground or some other age-appropriate place.

❤ Now you are free to consciously evoke the capable, resourceful adult in you to perform your difficult task. *Visualize* this side of you confidently stepping forward.

(See A-16 for Preparation Activities.)

VISUALIZATIONS

16

Dust Bunnies

Are you lying in bed, too tired to combat negative thoughts, memories or images? It's time to pull out your vacuum cleaner! Visualize a white or pleasantly colorful hose coming to you from some celestial or divine source, and run that nozzle all over your brain. Get in the corners and over the bumps. *Visualize* those negative thoughts, memories or images being sucked right out, and relax in a fresh, cleaned-out space. *Ahhhh!*

VISUALIZATIONS

Warm and Relaxed

Find a quiet place to sit or lie down, where you will not be interrupted for five or ten minutes. **Breathe deeply** in through your nose; release your breath slowly and completely, out through your pursed lips, as if you were blowing into a balloon. Repeat two more times. Visualize a bright light that you can use as a spotlight to shine on various parts of your body. Visualize a source of heat (the sun?) you could use to warm your body.

Beginning at the top of your head, picture the light and heat directed at the top of your head and say to yourself, "**The top of my head is warm and relaxed**." Imagine this warmth, and continue breathing fully as you move the light to the back of your head and repeat: "The back of my head is warm and relaxed." Slowly move this warm light over different parts of your body, repeating, "My _____ is warm and relaxed…" and letting yourself sink into that sensation. When you have finished, keep breathing deeply for another minute, then open your eyes.

The colleague who shared this **biofeedback exercise** with me writes, "when we are very tense, or in pain, our muscles tighten and restrict blood flow, particularly to the small capillaries in our head, hands and feet. This exercise gets the blood flowing again. People who have migraines often complain of cold hands before or during the headache. Once you become comfortable doing this exercise, you will find your extremities are warmer when you have finished."

VISUALIZATIONS

Coast

Speeding and frantic? Whoa!—your vehicle is going way too fast! *Take your foot off the accelerator.* Imagine that you lightly tap the brakes and shift into neutral. Coast off the road and onto the grassy verge—or, if you are in a city, the empty parking lot of a toy store (any store you like). Roll down your window and look around: name three colors that you see. Notice that there is a light, pleasant smell in the air, and cute little birds chirping in the trees. Take a deep breath and let your head loll back against the headrest. Close your eyes, put one hand over your heart and s-l-o-w-l-y pat it as your breathe. Take your time—there is no hurry right now. Let everything slow down.

To The Moon!

Lying in bed, agitated and unable to sleep? Imagine you are driving a car on a crowded street, through a shopping area, over a rubble-strewn construction site…it is stressful but you are driving well and now you have driven through and past all that, and the road is less crowded. The surface is pleasingly smooth and now there are trees and fields around you. You are driving in the countryside and the road is getting straighter, there are no other cars, and driving gets easier and easier. Now—how nice! Your car gently lifts off into the air, completely unimpeded, no friction or restraints—it's so easy now. You are pleasantly floating in the air, pulling away from earth, leaving all your cares behind. Now you are driving into the beautiful night sky, with stars sparkling, and you can do this for as long as you want—weightless, no restraints, smooth, peaceful, vast… and in your control. You can return anytime you want, but right now, this feels so good….

VISUALIZATIONS

Activities: Description

Activities engage the mind's problem solving skills. They galvanize the I-Can-Do-It Karate Master in you: she or he who fears **not** the pen, page or keyboard. Set aside ten minutes to **do** something about your anxiety. *Action stirs us out of helpless feelings.* Plan to do an *Activity* while you are alert: fresh and as rested as you can be. This is when your brain is best able to perform "executive functions", i.e. thinking and organizing. Thoughtful (not impulsive) activity reduces anxiety and opens the way toward creative solutions.

Anxiety Journaling

♥ Pause and take a look at what's been going on in your life. Identify major events of the past 24 hours, the past week, month or year. Write a list of five events that are contributing to your anxiety, so you can help yourself understand that it is not weird or "out of the blue" to feel this way.

♥ Create an "anxiety" diary. At the end of each day, pick a number from 1 to 10 that rates the level of anxiety of that day, and write it on a calendar. (If you are female, track your menstrual cycle on that calendar, as well, because it may affect your mood.) Note in a journal the date, your symptoms, what was going on at the time or just before that time, and look for a pattern. Be your own sleuth – for anxiety is not a random event. Even if you look at your family history and identify a genetic predisposition, there will be intensifying triggers. Some books on anxiety offer detailed charts that may be helpful to you in your sleuthing. Also remember to look for the pattern of the days when you did *not* feel anxious! What was happening differently then?

ACTIVITIES

1

Rational/ Irrational

Write a list of all your anxiety related thoughts. Then go through the list and identify which ones are **R**ational fears, and which are **I**rrational fears.

♥ For example, *"I don't have enough money to pay my taxes!"* might be an **R**.

♥ *"I can't do anything right!"* is surely an **I**.

Rewrite the list with just the **R** fears, and develop a statement or plan that addresses each. (For example, *"I'm going to examine my accounts and if I don't have enough money, I'm going to call the IRS and work out a payment schedule."*)

If the "**I**" list is bothering you, go through it and come up with corrective statements. (For example, *"Sometimes I do things right and even very well. No one does everything right all the time, and I can't expect that of myself."*)

Contain It

Write a list of things you are thinking about in an anxious or worrying way and physically place that list in an actual box or drawer or container before going to bed. When you start worrying, remind yourself: *"That's written down, so I won't forget it. I don't need to think about that now."* Some people like to think of the container as a "God box," so they are putting their list in the care of their deity. The important thing is that it is physically placed in a location that is out of *your* mind.

A Date to Worry

Pledge to spend 15 minutes worrying at a specific, realistic time tomorrow. Write it down in your schedule, on the calendar, on a note on the kitchen table, etc. When you start worrying in bed, remind yourself that you have a date for worrying, and so *you are not going to worry now*. Then, keep that date! If you don't, your inner Self will learn not to trust you. Teach yourself that you are reliable, for you. Set a timer for fifteen minutes, so your worry is contained. Write down your topics, journal about them, etc. Speak into a tape recorder if you don't like to write. Dedicating a time just to worry can ease the strain and move you forward toward helpful changes.

Relax Muscles

As you lie in bed to nap or sleep, do this exercise: start at your toes and gently contract and then relax them. Flex and then relax your feet. Slowly work your way up your legs and torso, gently contracting and then relaxing the muscles in each area of your body. Do your neck and head: face, forehead and (just a little wiggle) scalp. If you drift off before finishing, that's great. Many people find that this mental focus, combined with the physical release of relaxing muscles after gently contracting them, does the trick. (You may prefer to start at your head and work down.)

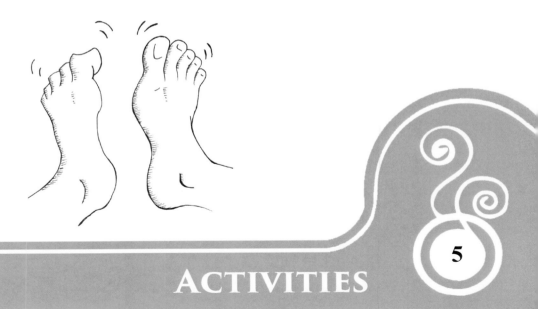

ACTIVITIES

Listen

Download or purchase a CD of visualizations, meditations, or stories designed to aid sleep. Listen to it, or play very soft and relaxing music (classical, jazz, New Age…). Studies show that accelerated respiration and heartbeat slow down as a person pays attention to gentle music. Auditory experiences influence our thoughts, transitioning them away from worrying topics. Be patient as you listen, and allow time (easily ½ hour or more) to gently unravel you toward sleep. Check 'Resources' on the website for samples of different types of music.

ACTIVITIES

6

Pizza, Anyone?

Think of yourself as a pizza pie! Draw the circle on a paper. *How big is the "anxiety" slice? What are the other slices?* How much space in your life is taken up with work, relationships, exercise, spirituality, special interests, family, etc? Different people have different sizes and categories of slices. Some people realize that their "anxiety" slice is pretty small, but maybe it's intense. Or maybe it is not a slice, but scattered over everything, like pepperoni on the pie. This exercise helps one gain a sense of proportion: *if it's a slice, then it is NOT all of me.* How can I strengthen the other aspects and reduce the size of this slice? If it's sprinkled all over the pie, *it's still not the foundation of who I am. And if it is the foundation (pie crust, pie pan), what is all this other yummy stuff?*

ACTIVITIES

Three Good Things

If you are kept awake by negative memories or thoughts about Self, break into them – disrupt them – by writing a list of *three things I did today about which I feel good*. It can be as simple as brushing your teeth, making a difficult phone call and feeding the dog. Or it can be quite complex, like three things you accomplished toward organizing a trip. Don't let your mind stray; stay focused on your list of three good things.

Laugh It Off

Anxious about a specific event, or caught in a life of ongoing anxiety? Born anxious? Well, reach for the comedies! Laughter is not simply a distraction—science shows that it releases into your bloodstream chemicals that shut down "fight or flight" activity in the brain. When this happens, you are able to think more clearly and perceive situations with greater accuracy. Humor is fun in the moment, enhances your perception and counters the negative effects of stress on your body. Read humorists, listen to comedians, watch comedies. Enjoy a laugh!

ACTIVITIES

Forgive

Consider forgiveness: some people find (to their surprise) that they can experience release from anxiety by forgiving. Write, *"I forgive…"* and see what comes next. *"myself for being imperfect"* can be a good one…, or *"my friend/ parent/ partner for saying* _____*"* might help. Practice forgiving, especially yourself, and see how that feels inside.

Aargh!

The worst-case scenario: why not face it? You're thinking about it anyway. Write down your worst fear.   (Mine involved me in a cardboard box in a gutter.)

♥ Write down an improvement—a possibility that is not as extreme. (Compared to our worst fear, everything is an improvement, right?)

♥ Write down a **reasonable** outcome, one that is okay with you. List what you would need to do in order to get there. What are your resources? Think about friends, relatives, organizations, free services, counselors, etc.

♥ What would you need to *invest*, in terms of money, energy and time? (*It may help to do A-2 "Rational/Irrational" as part of this.)

♥ The goal is to mobilize resources, because our worst fear is paralyzing. Grappling with the "worst-case scenario" strengthens us to face our demons and *think beyond them.*

Walk and Talk

Go for a walk *and speak your thoughts out loud*. (Yes, make sure no one is around, or speak quietly to yourself.) There is something about being in motion while getting our worries out of the stewpot of the head that often leads to greater clarity. Just hearing yourself *say what you are thinking* can bring insight. For, what comes to mind next? Does that sound 'right'? What else?

ACTIVITIES

Anyone There?

Talk with other people. You are not alone, so don't act alone. You never know who will say something helpful, or what they might say. Call, write, email, text a friend or friends, and request their help. Ask for a daily or weekly phone call, text message—whatever you need. Say, "I could really use your help right now" and describe what you would like. For many of us, it is so hard to ask—but it is vital, because asking for what we need makes it easier for others to know what to give, and tells our "inside self" that we can, indeed, advocate for ourselves.

What if you have no friends, or are ashamed of admitting to fear and loneliness, or are afraid of appearing weak? Negative riffs (no one cares; I'm such a loser; blah blah blah!) are so familiar. Don't fall for it. Not only are you wonderful, but also—there are good people everywhere: nurse at your doctor's office; person sitting next to you in church/ synagogue/ mosque; counselor at your local clinic, group at Al-Anon… But, sadly, none of them can read your mind. Therefore, as hard as it might be—and it might be the hardest thing you have ever done—speak up. Prove to yourself that you are here for you by asking for what you need.

And one more thing: some people may turn you down. They've got their reason, and most likely it's nothing to do with you. Be proud of having the strength to ask, and move on to the next person.

Once Upon a Time

Soothe the little kid in you by reading to yourself wonderful children's picture books that have beautiful or funny graphics. Ahhh! Before you go to bed, or in the afternoon with tea and a cookie (juice and a carrot?), let yourself relax into a simpler time. If life wasn't simple or you were never read to as a child, it's not too late now! Create this gentle oasis for yourself.

There's a list of potential books under 'Resources' on our website, to which I would love to add your favorite.

Good Things Journal

Review your Good Things (or Go To) Journal.

❤ *What is this?*

If you don't have one yet, I recommend that you start your own *Good Things Journal* right away. Suggested basic materials: 3 ring notebook and a box of page-size, clear sheet-protectors (cheap at Staples). Into these sheet-protectors, slide items that are healthy, healing, fun, funny, wise, pleasing, to you. For example: photos of people, animals, places that you love; inspirational quotes, cards from loved ones, cards you have bought yourself because they are so beautiful (don't forget to write yourself a love note in the card!); compliments people have given you, cartoons that tickle you, lists of how to take care of yourself, lists of people you admire and/or love, treasures found in nature such as feathers and leaves, etc. In other words, fill your *Good Things Journal* with *things that feel good!* Then it becomes a "Go-To" resource for hard times. (And you can continue to add to it for the rest of your life.)

Preparation Activities

Anxious about a task you must perform? ♥Along with *V-16*, prepare yourself by practicing what you want to say in front of the mirror, in the car and/or in front of a friend. Don't worry about memorizing exact language—just let yourself become familiar with speaking these thoughts out loud. ♥Write yourself an easy-to-read list of the most important points and add some encouraging words. Gather a good luck item or two, a photo of someone you love or an inspiring leader, and pick from your wardrobe your favorite clothes. ♥Just prior to the task, nip into a bathroom and assume the Superman or Wonder Woman stance for two minutes as you look over your notes. Remind yourself to smile (if appropriate), breathe (always appropriate), slow down (speak *low and slow*), sit back in your chair (if a chair is involved) and relax your hands. ♥Re-read your encouraging words, absorb the good energy from your talismans and photos, take several restorative breaths and center in your Adult Self. ♥Now you are ready. Go forth!

(Famous people have been known to cry, throw up, and/or have diarrhea as part of pre-speech or performance jitters—and then go on to do a great job. Take heart!)

ACTIVITIES

Observe and Accept

Observe. Get some internal distance by looking at what you are feeling, and then speak it to yourself: *Oh, this is fear! (pain, anger, jealousy, stress, etc.)* Objectively naming a feeling helps you not be engulfed by it, bumps you back and gives you a micro break from it. Then, *accept* it. "I accept that I am having fear." Otherwise you will expend energy fighting with reality—and that is truly an exhausting and futile activity. *Accepting* is an *active* process: *choose* to accept, rather than resist. *Accepting* is NOT the same as *surrendering, agreeing* or *approving*. *Accept*, because then what is happening can flow through you and not get stuck. *Observe* what happens in your body when you sincerely say, "I *accept* this fear." Is there a little shift? What happens to your shoulders, your breath?

ACTIVITIES

The "Not" List

List all your worries in a **not...right now** format. Examples:

I am **not** going to worry about my sister because she is getting help and she is okay, **right now.**

I am **not** going to worry about losing my job because I have the job, **right now.**

I am **not** going to worry about my health because a) I am doing many good things for it, b) test results so far are good, and c) there is nothing more I can do, given finances, **right now.**

I am **not** going to worry about talking to _____ because we are not having a conversation, **right now.**

I am **not** going to worry about my son/daughter because he/she is living his/her own life, it is in his/her hands, he/she is an adult, and there is nothing more I can do, **right now.**

I am **not** going to worry about money because there is nothing I can do about it, **right now.**

I am **not** going to worry about that embarrassing moment because it already happened, I lived through it, and it is not occurring, **right now.**

This may seem massively delusional and like advocating head-in-the-sand denial, but usually what we worry about is **not** happening *right now*. More often, it is something that happened in the past or something that may or may not happen in the future—it is **not** something that is going on in this instant, as you are preparing dinner or getting ready for bed. Free yourself by writing your "**not**" list. Put it in a drawer (ahh!) and focus your attention on whatever is happening, **right now.**

Keeping it Real

Remember: in order to improve outcome, you may need to reduce your expectations. What are you asking of yourself? Is it realistic, or modeled on a world of remorseless 'shoulds'? Pressure on self, or others, to be some form of *perfect*, just increases stress and self-doubt. Write down your expectations. How can you reduce them? Where can you let go?

♥ Imagine holding a measuring stick in your hand. Is it your measuring stick, or someone else's? What if you are "not measuring up" because it is the *wrong measuring stick?*

♥ Picture a horizontal bar that you are going to jump over. Is it at a realistic height? If you jump it, does it immediately move higher? *Who is setting that bar?* Maybe you need to *lower* it. Awakening to what is right, *for you and only you,* is vital to keeping it real.

ACTIVITIES

Active Meditation

Physical activity that has a lot of focus can be used as an active meditation. Think of an activity in which you may 'lose' yourself, such as gardening, preparing food, arranging flowers, painting a chair. Focus **only** on what you are doing: the movements, how your body feels, the texture of the soil, colors of food, smell of flowers, feeling of pulling a brush full of paint up the leg of a chair...

♥ If you are too anxious to focus, try chanting or walking while saying out loud affirmations that are an uneven number of syllables (3, 5, 7, 9). Thus you say a syllable or word with the forward movement of each foot, so that when you start saying it over again, you will be stepping out with the opposite foot: good for using both hemispheres of the brain. Ex: "I am strong and I can cope." "I am filled with gratitude." "This, here, now." Remember that even when you are in bed, you can be active internally via prayer and use of imagination.

Body Cues: Description

Body Cues are simple tips for easing stress as you feel it in your body. They are actions and attitudes that, with very little effort, can be built into your daily routine. Body Cues support awareness of your body as a beautiful ecosystem that is doing its best for you all the time.

Our culture emphasizes The Head, as if it is in control and can boss everything else around. We frequently treat the body as a slave, a display case, or simply as a podium for our heads. But in many ways, the body holds the key. It is the truthful 'first responder' that lets you know when something isn't right, whether you are ill or under emotional strain. Thus you must be gentle with your body and pay attention to its needs. Remember that when you are anxious, your body bears the brunt of your suffering (nausea, light-headed, pounding heart, dry mouth, etc). Your body deserves your loving care.

Limit Stimulants

Limit your intake of caffeine and any other stimulants. For example, I have to limit myself to two caffeinated teabags per morning, and no caffeine after noon. (I love strong tea, so this is not easy.) Anxiety asks that we *soothe* our nervous system, not increase its stimulation. Negative reactions to caffeine, etc. may include heart racing and palpitations. ("I'm having a heart attack!") As much as you love your brew, for the sake of your well-being, cut back.

Be Gentle

When you shower or bathe, make a conscious effort to be gentle. Think of your body as fragile and new, like a little child's, and wash yourself with that level of consideration. A period of anxiety is a period of travail—it is exhausting; there is torment suffered, even though the source may be from within. Conscious, gentle touch may bring comfort. Relax into the sensation as you gently smooth pleasing lotion over your skin. *Ahhh!*

♥ What else *gentles* you? Soft textures, soothing music, pleasing fragrances, candlelight? When anxious, a friend of mine likes to rock himself while wrapped in a soft blanket...

BODY CUES

2

Edit Exposure

Restrict and edit the TV and other media that you listen to and watch. Recognize that you are not immune to the stresses of the world around you. For this period of time, while you are helping yourself reduce anxiety, you may well benefit from limiting exposure to all its turmoil. *For sleep's sake, stay away from the evening news.* Remember, "the news" is only part of the picture—usually the frightening and negative part. There are acts of compassion, generosity, heroism and selflessness going on every day. While you are healing anxiety, be careful what you allow yourself to see, hear or read.

BODY CUES

Tension Release

Assess the level of tension in your body. Jaws clenched, back tight, knuckles white? Perhaps what is needed is *physical release:* walk briskly, run (screaming, if no one's around) through the woods, pound on pillows, kick empty boxes, throw rocks into a stream. (But don't do this in front of anyone who might burst out laughing, or else be frightened by your physical release. Explain yourself if another person is around.) City dweller? Scream into a pillow, consider a kick-boxing class, dance wildly to loud music (maybe with your head-set on). Sometimes I like to roar like a lion! *RRROAARR!!!* (*Ahh*: that felt good!)

Get that tension moving **out** of your body.

BODY CUES

Massage

If you can afford a massage, by all means, get one. If part of your anxiety is financial and paying for a massage would just add to it, there are other things you can do. *Exchange back, foot and/or neck rubs with a friend.* If isolation is part of the problem, or the idea of someone else touching you is 'icky', *place a tennis ball (any softish ball) between your back and the wall and gently press against it, moving around to work it into sore places.* I have mine in an old stocking so it doesn't drop. You'll probably be surprised at how many sore spots there are. *Lean your back against the edge of a doorframe and let it work into the muscles.* Knobs, corners, edges in your home may be used to **help** your body. There are low cost implements, both non-electric and electric, that can be quite helpful. Don't forget the potential help of hot and cold packs.

♥ Massage schools frequently have students who give free or nominally priced massages as part of their training—check your yellow pages.

Stretch

Stretch to relieve tension, and hold a stretch for at least thirty seconds to allow the message to enter muscle-memory. Fear and all its derivatives (anxiety, worry, stress, etc.) cause us to tighten our muscles. Gentle stretching is like telling yourself, *"It's okay; I can relax now."* There are excellent stretching books available, and gentle, affordable stretching and yoga classes. Restorative Yoga is specifically designed to facilitate peace in an anxious and /or depressed physical-emotional system.

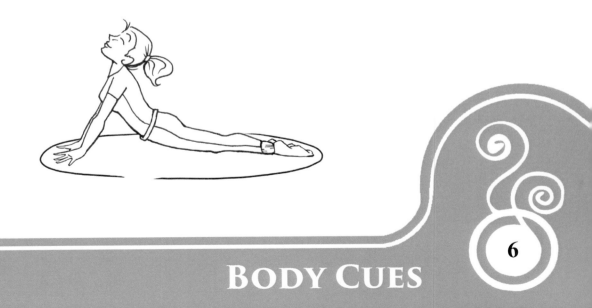

Nutrition

Good nutrition helps counteract anxiety. Stress burns up certain vitamins, so you may need to supplement your diet with quality vitamins. See a nutritionist, or research supplements in your local health food store, library or on the web. Check with your physician or pharmacist to ensure there are no contraindications for you.

♥ Our bodies are not all the same! If you can find a nutritionist who is skilled at tapping into your particular body (kinesiology, motility testing), rejoice! Chances are you will receive support that is customized to your needs.

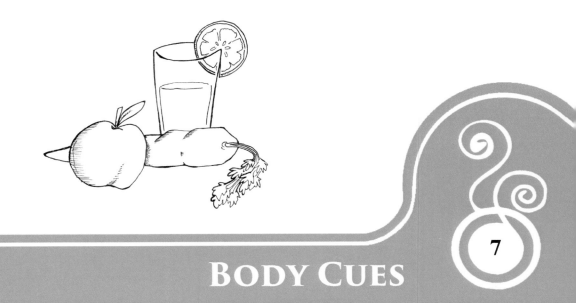

BODY CUES

Exercise

Regular exercise helps with anxiety and sleep. Exercise in any form releases anti-anxiety and antidepressant chemicals into the bloodstream, burns up stress chemicals and stimulates Ch'I (energy). Studies show that:

- ♥ a ½ hour walk three to four times a week stimulates production of the body's natural antidepressant.
- ♥ exercise that elevates the heart rate (brisk walk? Uphill?) *reduces anxiety and episodes of panic.*
- ♥ treadmills are great—but if you can walk outdoors (*ahh!*) you will receive extra benefit from the unexpected gifts of the natural world (see that chipmunk? Hear that bird? Smell that blossom? Feel that breeze?).

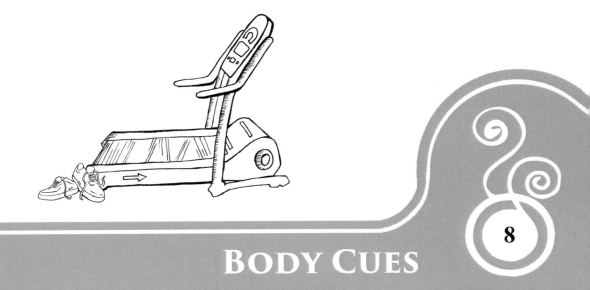

BODY CUES

Before Midnight

Biorhythms indicate that falling to sleep before midnight yields the best quality sleep. If possible, go to bed before midnight. Track back from when you have to get up in the morning, in order to figure out what time you need to go to bed. How many hours of sleep do you need? It's quite individual; some need six hours and others need nine. (Some studies show that we can compensate for missed sleep by sleeping like crazy at the end of an insomnia period.)

Three-hour Rule

Adopt the three-hour rule: don't eat a big meal or exercise strenuously less than three hours before bedtime. Either may interfere with sleep. A heavy meal may burden your metabolism, and strenuous exercise may boost your metabolism. A healthy snack is fine: nuts, cheese, yogurt, fruit, lean meat or tofu, baked potato, a bowl of soup…. Plan your snack with your individual needs in mind (food allergies, special diet, etc.).

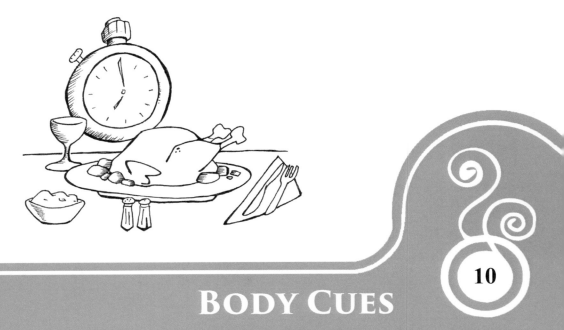

Sleep Routine

Develop a sleep routine: choose your bedtime to allow enough sleep, prepare the room in advance (darken the room, etc) so you do not have to **do** things as you get into bed. Consider: do I need an eye pillow to shut out light, ear plugs to shut out noise, good shades on the window? Is my mattress comfy? (You can add a comfortable layer to it.) Is there anything in the room that catches my eye in a disturbing way in the middle of the night? (Ex: reflection off a mirror. Try draping the mirror with cloth.) One-half hour before bedtime: wash face, brush teeth, take out contacts, put on PJ's, etc. Then do something relaxing for the rest of that ½ hour: drink herbal tea, read a light book, listen to soft music, watch gentle TV, pet the cat….

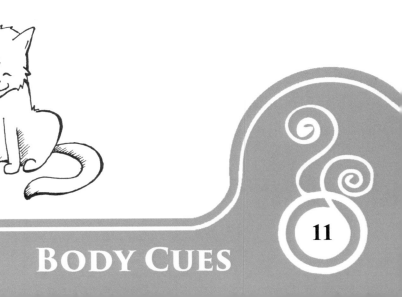

BODY CUES

Natural Sleep Aids

Consider natural sleep aids: research herbs in the library, on the web, at your local health food store. (Check with your physician or pharmacist to make sure there is no interaction with your medication.)

♥ The scent of *lavender* has been used to facilitate sleep for centuries. Sprinkle your pillow with lavender water, put a lavender sachet beneath it, add some drops of lavender oil to your before-bed bath.

♥ A friend of mine loves her eye-pillow (weighted with beads or grains). She says, "When it is draped across my eyes, I feel like somebody is taking care of me". *(Ahhhhh!)*

Soak Your Feet

Chinese medicine, which is at least two thousand years old, advises: soak your feet in warm water before going to bed in order to facilitate sleep. This helps because all the body's energy meridians end in the feet. Consider this additional information: 1) the body's largest pores are on the face and the soles of the feet. 2) blood circulates through the body, start to finish, in about two minutes. Some holistic practitioners advocate a periodic twenty-minute Epsom salt foot-bath (since you can't soak your face ♥) for its blood cleansing properties. What about other herbs? Add some lavender oil?

BODY CUES

Healing Hands

When anxious, what do you do with your hands? I rub mine together, fidget and pick at things. Many cultures and traditions incorporate *worry* stones, prayer beads or rosaries. Beyond the ineffable value of prayer, these items provide tactile focus that is soothing to the spirit.

♥ Carry in your pocket something smooth (or rough) to finger and roll in your hand during stressful times.

♥ Handcrafts, such as knitting, facilitate relief and create calm through their hypnotic, repetitive motion.

♥ Energy healers practice *laying on of hands*, believing that energy flows through the palms. Gently place your hands on any part of your body that is tense, and slowly breathe into this place.

♥ Sensations help us break out of obsessive worry and/ or escalating panic.
In a public setting, secretly run your thumb over the teeth of a key or a comb
in your pocket. In a private setting, wrap an ice cube in a washcloth and
hold it in one hand until it feels too cold, and then switch hands. Whether
pleasant or unpleasant, sensation gets the brain's attention, thus pulling
it away from escalating anxious thoughts.

Slow Down

Be aware that anxiety renders some people accident-prone. Whether it's from being preoccupied and therefore inattentive, or *racing* and thus moving too quickly, the body is likely to suffer dings and bangs: a stubbed toe, banged head, slip on the stairs, fender-bender. If you assess yourself as anxious, **slow down.** Remind yourself of the parameters of your body (*keep in touch*). Use sensation to help you stay present: put a rubber band on your wrist and periodically snap it; splash cold water in your face. Start the day with clapping your hands and stamping your feet. Let sensation help you get grounded.

BODY CUES

Great Grounding

"Grounding" is an essential tool for slowing down the racing tempo of anxiety. Happily, it is simple: just grab a chair and sit down. Now close your eyes and concentrate on the sensation of your weight sinking down onto the seat of the chair. *(Ahh. I'm here!)* What does it feel like on your butt and thighs? What about the weight on your feet? Wiggle your toes and grind your heels into the floor. Lean back and feel the support of the chair on your back. Clench your fists tightly and then relax your hands in your lap or on the arms of the chair. How does that feel? Ideally it is pleasant to loosen your muscles and let your weight sink down onto a strong, supportive, surface. Gravity pulls you toward the Earth, and the Earth is our ultimate support. If you are anxious while sitting on the bus or in a meeting, focus on the sensation of where your butt, back and thighs rest on your seat and where your feet (wiggle your toes) rest on the floor. Let yourself feel thick and heavy: get physically grounded.

BODY CUES

90 Seconds

A burst of emotion is experienced via body-produced chemicals that flush through the system in only ninety seconds. After that, you can continue re-stimulating those chemicals by repeating stressful thoughts and images, OR you can say—*Wow! I don't like how that felt!* –and choose not to repeat (dwell on) the thought. **Yes!** Doing this is much harder than it sounds. Please forgive yourself in advance for not being able to successfully drag your thoughts away from certain stress images or sequences, time and again. Help yourself interrupt the repetition of stressful thoughts and images by saying, "**drop it!**" out loud or to yourself. Snap a rubber band on your wrist, visualize a STOP sign—anything that acts as a "reset" button for your mind.

BODY CUES

The Nose Knows

Smell is the most basic of our five senses. Odors that are associated with difficulty and pain can trigger or heighten anxiety, while scents that are associated with pleasure can reduce it. Identify odors that increase your anxiety (for me, gasoline is one such smell). Bring conscious awareness to difficult smells: "I know what is happening; I'm smelling gasoline, and it is triggering me." Awareness reduces the physiological out of control sensations that flood us when we are triggered.

Pleasurable and soothing scents can help us transition out of anxiety by reminding us of better times, or pressing a sensory 'reset' button. A friend of mine loves the scent of citrus, which is available in natural air sprays. Nice! I like the scent of vanilla, coffee beans, flowers and freshly mown grass. What about the smell of the ocean, or the air just before and after it rains? Rummage in your memory banks (that great storehouse) for your soothing aromas. Close your eyes and vividly recall an enjoyable scent.

BODY CUES

Breathe

Don't forget to *breathe!* It's so essential, and so forgettable. Start the day with three deep breaths. ♥Lie on the bed or floor and breathe in until your belly rises (the lower lungs are filled); breathe out slowly and when you feel empty, blow out three more short bursts (to really empty the lungs). Or, ♥press your back and shoulders against the wall as you breathe in, then bend over slightly while exhaling—and slow it down by shaping your lips as if you are blowing through a straw. Exhaling twice as long as you inhale *cues* the body's "soothing" parasympathetic system—as does bending forward as you exhale. Observe how many times during the day you catch yourself holding your breath. *Remind yourself to breathe.* Stick 'post-its' on the bathroom mirror, computer monitor, car dashboard, refrigerator.

Nice breathing mantras: *breathe in the rose* (inhale), *blow out the candle* (exhale).
Breathe in: *present moment.* Breathe out: *pleasant moment.*

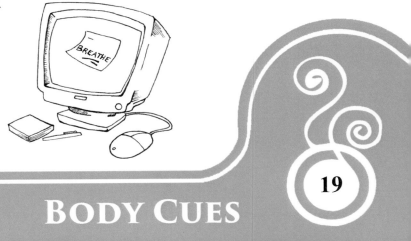

BODY CUES

This. Here. Now.

Metaphorically, wrap yourself snugly in this moment and attend to what is immediately in front of you. Don't go with racing, futuristic thoughts because right now, while they are anxiety fueled, they are not helpful. As they say in the Recovery movement, "Keep your head where your feet are." Think solely in terms of what is the immediate next thing to take care of: think brief and small. *This. Here. Now.* Simple tasks bring relief, like cleaning out the crumbs in the utensil drawer or scrubbing tile grout with a toothbrush. Keep it simple, keep it small. Organize your shoes, or the medicine cabinet, or your wallet, or your socks. Be proud of yourself for accomplishing small, simple things.

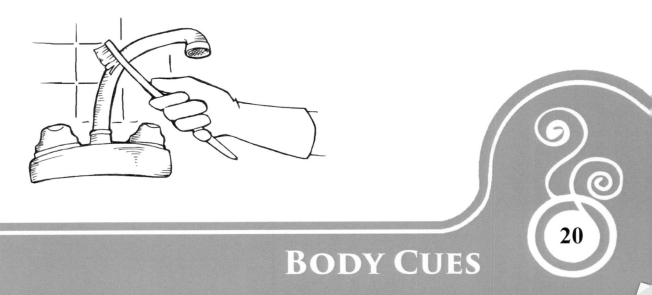

BODY CUES

"Some days, the Dragon wins."

Sometimes NOTHING works. Accept this ("suffering is pain plus lack of acceptance"). If you are unable to sleep, get up, read, take a hot bath, listen to soft music, drink hot milk—whatever. And pledge to set yourself up for sleep the following night as best you can. For a period of time, you may need sleeping medication: see your doctor and let him or her know that you've been working on this issue in other ways, but right now you need the extra help. (Please do not overuse alcohol in an effort to get sleep. It will backfire on you, causing other problems.)

Let us acknowledge that it is really hard to be calm when a relationship is falling apart, you are living in some form of demeaning or frightening abuse or suffer flashbacks of past abuse. It's natural to be tense when you have survival worries (job, food, home), unwanted isolation or too much responsibility (i.e. single parenting with a full time job, no helpful relatives nearby). How can you relax when there is chronic or serious illness within you or a loved one, or when you are in pain? So many real life situations make it truly difficult to quiet and comfort yourself. Yet, at the very least, you can improve moments for yourself.

And that's your job: to figure out how to take care of yourself, so that you can have a good life. Where are your moments of calm, and how can you expand them? What thoughts fan the fire, and what thoughts relax you? How do you soothe your harried self, reassure your frightened self, calm your raging self? How can you use your thoughts to help, and not harm, yourself?

Anxiety, at a level that interferes with your ability to sleep or function during the day, can be a remorseless agent for growth. Take heart! Sufficient discomfort may lead to seeking out inner resources, breaking old habits, developing skills and, ultimately, deepening your relationship with yourself.

> "Most people don't recognize opportunity when it comes, because it's usually
> dressed in overalls and looks a lot like work."
> —*Thomas Edison*

INFORMATION

Addendum

Get a Physical
It is important to see your physician for a physical, and describe your symptoms to him or her. Thus you can verify to yourself that it is NOT an illness—you are physically 'safe'. Then you can focus on dealing with your anxiety—and that may include temporarily taking anti-anxiety medication.

Perimenopausal and Menopausal Women: Heart palpitations are part of the saga of menopause for many women, and can cause a great deal of anxiety. Get yourself checked out medically, and consult a holistically minded practitioner who specializes in this life passage. Then you will be able to feel physically assured as you work with your anxiety.

Everyone: Don't forget valuable holistic medical resources: acupuncture and Chinese medicine, homeopathy, naturopathy, chiropractics, osteopathic manipulation, etc.

Feelings and the Body: Although deep breathing and stretching are universally acknowledged to be healthy, some people resist them. Recent science (and ancient wisdom) suggests that *feelings* are 'stored' in tense muscles, and may be released during these processes. For example, some people are surprised to find themselves welling up with tears during a gentle stretching class. (Could this be due to the kind voice of the instructor? What tone of voice do you use, when you speak to yourself?) Deep breathing may stir feelings, as well. Don't be afraid of your feelings even if they surface at an inconvenient time. They are healthy and normal, and present for a reason.

Hello, Cynic!

Life experience, and some schools of childrearing, may support the development of a robust internal Cynic. That's the sneering, lip-curled aspect of self that says, "This is dumb— no way I'm doing this!" or "Yeah, right! No way this is going to help!" I think the Cynic is a defense against vulnerability—that tender shoot of hope that has been trampled underfoot too many times, and fears disappointment yet again. If you were raised in the "*I'll give you something to cry about!*" school of childrearing, you'll probably have defenses that may get in the way of trying these resources. Similarly, if you were raised in the "*stray cat*" school of childrearing (*don't get underfoot and I'll leave out some milk*), a sense of unworthiness may enfeeble your efforts on your own behalf. If you are about to set this book aside unused, ask yourself,

"Is this my 'Cynic'?
Do I really want this aspect of myself to make this decision for me?"

You **do** have a choice.

Anxiety Soothers and Psychotherapy

The techniques described in **Anxiety Soothers** are intended as "self-help" and cannot be used in place of counseling and psychotherapy. These techniques are not designed to get at deep, underlying issues, and sometimes it is vital to get at those unresolved issues in order to gain relief. For that level of work, please consult a reputable therapist or counselor.

Anxiety Soothers and Meditation

Meditation: what a wonderful thing, and how perplexing to our busy Western minds. **Observe and Accept** (A-17) is a vital part of the meditative practice of *Mindfulness*. Other techniques (V-6, 10 & 14; A-5 & 20, B-19 & 20) may be used as *Active Meditations*. Practice with these, and by all means pursue any form of meditation toward which you are drawn. Just five minutes a day of non-judgmental focus on something simple, such as breathing, can be restful and soothing for your entire system. Meditation helps you stay in the present moment rather than worrying about the future or fretting over the past. Its mental focus leads to diminished anxiety—but don't stress yourself about doing it "right". *Relax, drop all "shoulds", and just be.*

Free meditation groups and inexpensive meditation classes may be found in most communities. Meditation instructions are available via the web, books, CDs, Apps and Retreats at meditation centers.

Sympathetic (SNS) / Parasympathetic (PNS)

Brace yourself for a watered-down dose of important neuroscience! The brain and the body are inextricably interwoven via neurochemical interactions that create our sense of dis-ease and wellness. You can use this knowledge to help *calm* your system.

The sympathetic (SNS) and parasympathetic (PNS) nervous systems are two major players in this interweave. When there is a threat or crisis, imagined or real, the sympathetic nervous system (SNS) releases into the bloodstream "fight or flight" neurochemicals. If these neurochemicals are continually present due to chronic stress, they are potentially physiologically damaging. They block access to the "rest and digest" parasympathetic nervous system (PNS), which is responsible for releasing into the bloodstream the calming and stabilizing neurochemicals that further a sense of contentment and relaxation. Because the two systems are mutually exclusive—i.e., when one is "on", the other is pretty close to "off"—it is vital in our stressed lives to learn how to turn "on" the PNS.

Effort is involved because our fear-evoking SNS is constantly stimulated by scary news, fear-inducing advertisements and frightening TV shows or movies. Media take advantage of the fact that we are biologically 'wired' (from primitive times when humans were potential prey) to be vigilant for danger. Quieting down our reactivity to this constant barrage, along with the stressful events occurring in our own lives, is vital to creating calm in our own precious eco-systems. *Visualizations*, *Activities* and *Body Cues* contribute toward activating the PNS and thus soothing the entire system: your body, your mind, your thoughts and finally, your life. *Ahh.*

About the Author

Jeremy Cole, MSW, LCSW, began her life as a psychotherapist in 1995. While her therapeutic 'home' is the rich, relational world of AEDP (Accelerated Experiential Dynamic Psychotherapy), she continues to explore evolving psychotherapeutic approaches and the integration of emergent information about the brain. Acutely respectful of the suffering caused by anxiety, this book started many years ago with ideas scribbled on scraps of paper during a long and relentlessly anxious passage in her own life. She may be reached at:

anxietysoothers@gmail.com

About the Illustrator

Dani Lee Croasdale holds a BFA in Illustration and Art Education from the Maine College of Art. She lives in Portland, Maine, and works as an illustrator, graphic designer and computer consultant on projects nationwide. Dani enjoys collaborating on creative projects with enthusiastic people who share her ideals and passions. For further information, she may be reached at:

danicroas@gmail.com

7

INFORMATION

www.anxietysoothers.com

This book is intended to be a helpful, easy-to-use guide that will lead you to a peaceful day and a good night's sleep. The interactive **Anxiety Soothers** website (**www.anxietysoothers.com**) offers a few more *Visualizations*, *Activities* and *Body Cues* for your relaxation and enjoyment as well as audio versions of each. It also includes references for information in the book, a portal to further resources, information about the Anxiety Soothers App, and anything else helpful as it comes across my desk. In other words, I imagine it growing and developing past what I can envision as this book goes to print! I welcome your helpful suggestions and while I'll appreciate all of them, I will post the ones that seem particularly useful on the **www.anxietysoothers.com** Comments page.

Thanks to my clients, who teach me a great deal about living.
Thanks to Life for providing me with enough unbearable anxiety
to spur desperate efforts to reduce it.
Thanks to Deborah Ann Light, who always backed me up,
and the wonderful people of the Writing Group:
Ann Marie, Kate, Martha, Rick and Joanna.
Thanks to dazzling colleagues:
Tom, Ann, Mark, Merle, Rick, Ramona, Chris and Ann Marie.
Thanks to family, especially my creative and colorful, one-and-only,
sunshiny, almost-twin sister Cambria,
and friends, especially Nancy, Ann, Tom, Charlotte, Cheryl and Carol.
Thanks to libraries, books in general, nature and especially
(but not exclusively) the ocean, lakes and forests of Maine and Washington State.
Thanks for every smile of kindness I have ever received,
and every helping hand (there have been so many).

INFORMATION

Purchasing your own copy of Anxiety Soothers:

Order from our website at www.anxietysoothers.com and get free shipping Media Mail.

For information about bulk purchases of **Anxiety Soothers** (parent groups, psychotherapy groups, schools, businesses, health care practices, etc), or for arranging in-service trainings and speaking engagements, please contact Jeremy Cole MSW, LCSW, through the website or at **anxietysoothers@gmail.com**.

Thank you! All blessings to you.

Jeremy